ronankeating
by Courtney Myers

Copyright © 1999 Omnibus Press.
(A Division of Book Sales Limited)

Cover & book designed by
Michael Bell Design.
Picture Research by Nikki Russell.

ISBN 0.7119.7659.7
Order No. OP 48137

Exclusive Distributors:
Book Sales Limited
8/9 Frith Street,
London W1V 5TZ, UK.

Music Sales Corporation
257 Park Avenue South,
New York, NY 10010, USA.

Five Mile Press
22 Summit Road,
Noble Park,
Victoria 3174, Australia.

To the Music Trade only:
Music Sales Limited
8/9, Frith Street,
London W1V 5TZ, UK.

Photo credits:
Front cover: Rex Features.
All other pictures supplied by
All Action, LFI, Redferns &
Rex Features.

Every effort has been made
to trace the copyright holders of
the photographs in this book but
one or two were unreachable.
We would be grateful if the
photographers concerned would
contact us.

Printed in the UK by
Printwise (Haverhill) Ltd., Suffolk.

A catalogue record for this book is
available from the British Library.

Visit Omnibus Press at
www.omnibuspress.com

ronankeating

by Courtney Myers

OMNIBUS PRESS

ronankeating

The Irish have built a nation on the strength of family ties. Though the young have traditionally left the Emerald Isle in search of fame and fortune, they never lose their links with hearth and home. And, more often than not, they return to the mother country to enjoy the fruits of their labours.

Pop's top boy band, Boyzone, launched their bid for world stardom in 1994 with their first single – and, having scaled both the international and Irish charts, celebrated their fifth year in the spotlight with a 'Greatest Hits' album that showcased every facet of their talents. Though the likes of 911, Five, Backstreet Boys and Another Level had followed successfully in their wake, their biggest rivals Take That had long since split into several solo factions, leaving the Boyz the decade's longest-lasting harmonising heart-throbs. Not bad for a group pulled together by a newspaper ad…

The reason Boyzone survived and thrived where others had fallen by the wayside was a real family feeling, from the youngest to oldest member. For lead singer Ronan Keating, youngest in both the group and his family of five children, the secret of Boyzone's success was simply to keep smiling. "I used to try to keep out of my brothers' arguments," he once said, "and I think it's really helped me 'cos now I don't get over-stressed about things."

And why should he worry? At the age of just 21, he'd been hailed as a singer, songwriter and all-round sex symbol, his earnings already in the seven-figure bracket. A second career as a TV personality was booming, while back in Dublin's fair city he'd installed his fashion model wife in a modern mansion and was just about to fill the nursery with the first of (doubtless) many blond-haired, blue-eyed offspring. A success story in anyone's book…

It was a story that had begun in Swords, Dublin on 3 March 1977 when bouncing Ronan John Patrick was born to proud parents Gerry and Marie Keating. They'd already produced three boys and a girl, and this child was to be the last of the brood. By all accounts, the new arrival was a dream child: "I was always known in my family as 'Little Ro'," Ronan blushes today. "At least it meant I was very spoiled… especially on my birthday and when Christmas came round!"

"I was always known in my family as 'Little Ro'"

Dad worked for a bottling factory, while Mam owned a hairdressing salon – which may or may not account for Ronan's *Smash Hits* – acclaimed hairstyle in later life! His first childhood memory dates from a family holiday in 1982, when he was brave enough to go horse-riding. Ronan didn't fall off his mount, but he proved a little accident-prone at other times: he still has a scar on his left arm from boiling water, a knife cut on the right arm and a series of bumps on his head from when "a rock fell on me."

A somewhat timid child, Ronan used to be terrified of the dark and found it hard to sleep with the lights off. "But I grew out of it when we moved to the country – there were no street lights!" The city boy had more to cope with than just the pitch-black nights when the Keatings exchanged Ireland's capital city for small-town Dunshaughlin, in County Meath. Pitched battles were the order of the (school) day: "Some of the boys didn't like me, 'cos I was from Dublin," Ronan remembers. "They ganged up on me but I sorted them out."

While learning to fight his corner, Ro had to be certain news of his escapades didn't reach home. "I wouldn't say my upbringing was strict," he's commented in the past, though he admits "We knew our place... when to say things and when not to." The dutiful son has since grown up to become a well-rounded human being and outstanding ambassador for pop.

But it wasn't easy to settle in Dunshaughlin, the kind of place people grew up in and remained all their lives; outsiders stayed outsiders for many years. As a child, Ronan would help his dad deliver goods to stores in local villages and got along well with shopkeeper's daughter Yvonne Connolly, a name that would crop up again later in his life...

He might have been a hit with the girls, but Ronan and school most certainly did not mix: four o'clock couldn't come quickly enough for the youngest Keating: "I liked the drama lessons, but that was only once a week." Until he joined Boyzone, Ronan once joked, "The highlight of my career as a performer was directing a play and playing a donkey in a nativity play!" Maths was a big turn-off and, because there weren't any PE lessons, fitness freak Ronan used to go jogging in lunch breaks. "Everyone thought that was very strange!"

But there was method in his madness; Ro was in fact a promising athlete, and had things turned out differently could have been gracing our TV screens on *Grandstand* rather than *Top Of The Pops*. "I was on the Irish youth team for four years," he reveals, modestly forgetting to mention an All-Ireland Championship title and wins at 200, 400 and 800 metres. He was even offered a scholarship for a four-year course in New York which could have led to a place on the Olympic squad – "But the band came along first." Brother Gerard had the same ambition, though a broken leg crushed his dream; he would later make his fortune on the American stock exchange.

As far as a 'normal' career went, Ronan wasn't into stocks and shares: he looked no further for a role model than his grandfather and uncle, both policemen. "Then I became really interested in security, and was going to study it for two years in college. It's funny that I now have security people working for me!"

But Boyzone, of course, was soon to change any ideas of a 'normal' career. One of the last options to surface before fame came calling was to join sister Linda in the States and work as a waiter in her diner. Bar work might well have followed… and it's not too hard to imagine Ronan doing the Tom Cruise *Cocktail* thing! But his main aim was to get out into the big, wide world as quickly as possible.

"All I wanted was to be able to leave school, I hated it that much," he remembers. "I wanted my mam to say, 'Yes, you can leave.' But of course she didn't want me to. That was hard, because I needed my mam's approval – I wouldn't have left if she hadn't come around to the idea."

For the time being, Ronan had to make do with odd jobs outside school hours, the first being part-time in a shoe shop. "I remember getting my first wage packet when I was about 15 and going with the lads to the Zoo Bar," he recalls. But everyday life didn't have many attractions for a kid with his head in the clouds, looking at the stars. "I always wanted to make something of my life, I was afraid of being a nobody or working a 9-5 job."

The opposite sex was also accounting for a growing part of his attention, not to mention any pocket money he made. His first girlfriend was called Rebecca. "We grew up in the same neighbourhood and nothing ever really happened. We didn't kiss or anything, we were just two young friends having a laugh, but we saw each other as boyfriend and girlfriend. Then I moved away and we never saw each other again."

His first kiss came at the ripe old age of 13: "I didn't know what was going on, but she did. It frightened the life out of me, but I think everyone feels like that the first time." We don't know who the lucky lady was, or her qualifications to give lessons in love – but, suffice to say, Ronan was a quick learner!

In terms of other temptations, he caught on fast too. Legend has it that he had his first, forbidden taste of the demon alcohol in the company of 18 year-old brother Gary – three pints of dark, creamy Guinness that made him as sick as a dog! Little wonder he's been known for his moderate habits since, and is a confirmed non-drinker even today.

"All I wanted was to be able to leave school, I hated it that much"

Despite being unable to get into his local church choir (really, some people have no taste!), Ronan sang in a few local bands before linking up with Boyzone, and this gave him an appetite for showbiz. "I always wanted to do something with my life that was in the public eye, whether it be sports or entertainment… I got the taste and wanted more." His young idols had been teen-pop duo Bros (he'd been especially smitten by their 1988 chart-stormer 'Cat Among The Pigeons') and cool cat Matt Goss, one half of Bros, would later become a pal. But Ro's last pre-Boyzone band, a heavy rock combo, were keener on grunge idols Nirvana than the soul music their singer loved, and a parting of the ways soon happened. "I'd *love* to meet up with them again," he says, "I know they're still playing."

Ronan's big break was getting into Boyzone – but it took all of three auditions for him to impress manager Louis Walsh, whose advert in the press for "good looking, talented young males who want to be famous" had inspired no fewer than 300 applicants. Stephen Gately, Shane Lynch and Keith Duffy were among those to make the grade, little knowing they'd soon be gazing from the bedroom walls of many thousands of fans the world over. And Ronan would play a vital role in helping that dream become reality.

While others attempted to impress with disco anthems, the audition number Ronan chose was very different – 'Father And Son'. A gentle ballad that brought out the best in his high, plaintive voice, the track was written by the London born singer-songwriter Cat Stevens and first released by him in 1971. It was a song about the gap between generations, with timeless, heartfelt lyrics. At the end of that audition, Louis was so impressed that he earmarked the song as a future group release, and after hiding away on the B-side of their Irish début it would emerge to become their fourth and (at the time) biggest UK hit.

Boyzone's rise to fame was both meteoric and against the odds. How so? Anyone who saw the TV clip of their very public first appearance on Irish TV will know what we mean. Gay Byrne, the grey-haired host of the *Late Late Show*, presented six young men (yes, there were six then) who paraded self-consciously in front of the cameras. Ronan was at the very end of the line in a flat cap (his grandfather's?) worn back to front, plus a rather daft sleeveless T-shirt. And if he seemed somewhat less than confident, maybe that's because this all happened just a day after he'd joined. "We had no routine, no choreographer and we weren't even friends," he now recalls. "We were *pathetic*!" Know what? He's right!

"I always wanted to do something with my life that was in the public eye"

The TV clip, which is now destined to make numerous unwelcome (but amusing) reappearances on TV out-take shows, gave Marie Keating no reassurance whatsoever that leaving school before taking his final exams had been a sensible course of action. "My mother thought I was mad joining a band," he says of the parental opposition he encountered. "At the beginning she didn't know what her teenage son was getting into. She was scared, thinking that the music business was all drugs and drinking."

It wasn't as if Ronan was the undisputed lead singer, either. The first song chosen for release – in Eire only – was 'Working My Way Back To You', an oldie first recorded by close-harmony group the Four Seasons in the 1960s and soulfully revived the following decade by the Detroit Spinners. It was Boyzone's chance to give it their distinctive touch... but when it came out, Stephen and Mikey were the featured vocalists, leaving Ronan to chip in on the chorus harmonies.

He claims not to have been jealous at this, but admits "It made me realise more that I did want to sing – so I was lucky to get the second single." That single was 'Love Me For A Reason', and that's where the success story started on the other side of the Irish Sea.

"My mother thought I was mad joining a band"

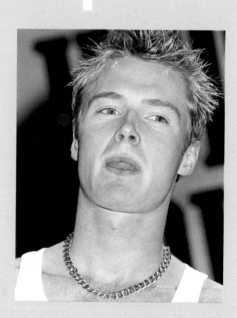

The line-up had been finalised when Mikey Graham was chosen to replace Mark and Richard, two of the original six who left soon after their TV début. With all five members now firmly in place, 'Working My Way...' had been released in late May of 1994 and was soon its way towards the top of the Irish charts. The highest rung would remain stubbornly out of reach thanks to the year's two biggest sellers – Wet Wet Wet's 'Love Is All Around' and the theme from *Riverdance*. Even so, it was a mighty impressive achievement for five unknowns...

'Love Me For A Reason' was a song that everyone could appreciate, having already been a hit back in 1974 for American boy band The Osmonds. So mums were singing along with daughters as harmony bridged the generation gap... for three short minutes, at least! The track which gave Ronan his first shot at the lead vocalist role very nearly went all the way to the top. Having reached Number 2 in style, the Boyz entered the Top 3 twice more in the spring and summer of 1995 with 'Key To My Life' and 'So Good', two original songs that proved – unlike some bands we could mention – that Boyzone didn't have to rely on cover versions for their hits.

"If I'm the highest-profile male in pop, then I'm honoured and flattered"

The band's big live break had come in 1994 in the shape of the *Smash Hits Show On The Road* – a package tour of pop hopefuls in which the Boyz took just six days to blossom from unknowns to headline attractions. Little wonder they were voted Best New Act in the annual poll that followed, playing the Poll Winners Party to 20,000 adoring females! They enjoyed the *Show On The Road* experience so much that they did the same tour the following year, and the magazine and its readers have always proved suitably grateful when it comes to handing out both column inches and accolades.

Producer Ray Hedges was the man selected to introduce the lads to the recording studio, and the evidence of *Said And Done* suggests it was a marriage made in heaven. Boyzone's first album hit the shops in late summer 1995, entering the charts at Number 1 – an outstanding feat for a new group, and sure evidence of their fast-growing popularity. Even Paul Weller and Supergrass had to bow to the Boyz! 'Father And Son' was the perfect Christmas single and made Number 2 late in 1995, only the unlikely combination of Robson and Jerome and then Michael Jackson holding it off top spot.

The Number 4 success of 'Coming Home Now' in the following spring meant that all five of Boyzone's British singles had reached the Top 5 – impressive by any standards. Their faces could be seen beaming from the covers of all the mags that mattered, though the cameras seemed to have fallen in love with one in particular.... Concerts saw 'We Love You Ronan' placards sprouting in the stalls, and pop pundits were openly talking about a potential solo career for one of the undisputed nice guys of pop.

By the time the *Smash Hits* Awards of 1996 came round, Boyzone had become fixtures. But Ronan was now being singled out for special treatment, winning no fewer than three categories in his own right – Best Male, Best Dressed Male Pop Star and Best Haircut. He played down the fact that fans were singling him out when the magazine interviewed him early in '97, saying simply: "We were and always will be equal in my eyes, but over the years it's just built up. I didn't look for it, it just happened. If I'm the highest-profile male in pop, then I'm honoured and flattered."

Amazingly, 'Little Ro' had emerged from being the youngest Boyzone member to become their unofficial leader. He was nine months the junior of second youngest Shane, while Mikey was a mighty four-and-a-half years his senior. There was little doubt where the spotlight was shining when the Boyz' cover of the classic Bee Gees ballad 'Words' gave them their first UK Number 1 in October 1996, a success repeated two months later with the exotic rhythms of 'A Different Beat', title track of the second Boyzone album. It would be the first of three consecutive Top 3 singles that Ronan had a hand in writing – proof that this was by no means a guy who relied on his face for his fortune.

But being attractive *was* an important part of the package. Back in the old days, male pop stars were supposed to be available – in other words, have no steady partner to put off hero-worshipping 'girlies'. John Lennon of The Beatles, for instance, had to conceal his marriage for fear fans would tear the lucky girl limb from limb. That was in 1963... and judging by the secrecy surrounding Ronan's relationship with Eternal member Vernie Bennett, it would seem little had changed in three decades. Coincidentally, his Boyzone buddy Shane was dating Vernie's sister Easther in an equally discreet fashion. Ro had met his future love backstage at a Dublin fashion show: a double date followed, setting a year-long relationship in motion.

While most pop stars are noted for their free and easy ways, the chief Boyzone boy's views on the sanctity of marriage had already inspired 'Ronan The Virgin' headlines. "A one-night stand isn't something that interests me at all," he said. "To me, sex is something you save for marriage, for that one person you will spend the rest of your life with."

In that respect it seemed Vernie was the ideal partner, since she also came from a strongly religious background. But they were to call it quits early in 1997, after which a newly free Ronan played the field... in a gentlemanly way, of course! He was seen out and about with Claire Danes, the lucky lady who played opposite Leonardo Di Caprio in the modernised version of *Romeo And Juliet*, but would only admit to being good friends with her.

Whatever the truth, it was all a long way from the girl called Georgina who he'd been dating when he first fell in with Boyzone. She'd apparently felt left out because the band's success took her fella away – and the memory of the rejection that followed hurt Ronan for many months. That said, many thousands of adoring female fans who listened to 'Isn't It A Wonder', Boyzone's first chart single of 1997 (and a Number 2 at that) would have been happy to be 'just good friends' with the boy of their dreams...

Ireland had laid claim to the Eurovision Song Contest long before Terry Wogan started doing the voice-over commentary – from 1970, in fact, when Dana brought back the crown with 'All Kinds Of Everything'. The winning streak had become even more pronounced in the 1990s, and when Dublin hosted the event yet again in 1997 a different slant was sought. Ronan was invited to front the show, and was flattered to be asked. His successful début as a TV 'talking head' would lead to a similar role at the MTV Awards... the only potential embarrassment being that he might have to present a trophy to himself!

"A one-night stand
isn't something that interests
me at all"

As Ronan took his first steps towards small-screen stardom, another familiar (though rather less handsome) face was coming his way. At first glance, the names Ronan and Rowan are just a letter apart – but the contrast between our Ro and Rowan 'Mr Bean' Atkinson was rather more marked! Neither could have known, though, that when Ronan was invited to co-write the theme song for Rowan's new film *Bean* he would end up with a prestigious award for his mantelpiece. 'Picture Of You' was the song, and it also titled a video collection that found itself in many fans' Christmas stockings as 1997 ended.

The other advantage of the 'Bean' link was the success of the rubber-faced character's film in the States. Ronan appreciated that being the lead track on the soundtrack album would help Boyzone's prospects there, and also paid tribute to the Spice Girls for "opening the door for pop in America… though we're doing something completely different." Were Boyzone to become household names on that side of the Atlantic, one unfortunate side-effect would be Ronan losing the ability to shop and socialise without being mobbed. "Even U2 could walk down the road here and not get noticed," he quipped. Ironically, in 1998, Boyzone would guest on Bono and Co's video for 'The Sweetest Thing'… filmed in what looked suspiciously like an American street parade!

Boyzone's chart progress had continued apace with the Number 2 success of 'Picture Of You', written by Ronan and Absolute, the production team behind the Spice Girls' success. Yet having scored with a hat-trick of self-penned singles, many were surprised when Boyzone released a version of Tracy Chapman's 'Baby Can I Hold You' in November 1997. It was a song many fans' parents might have had in their collections, having been aired on the American singer-songwriter's chart-topping album of nine years earlier. As it turned out, the song not only won them many new fans but pointed to the new, mature approach they would be pursuing from now on.

The year of 1998 started for Ronan as many have – in the studio, adding the final touches to a new album. But come February, he received the quite unexpected accolade of being voted Male Spectacle Wearer of the Year. Specs appeal? Phwooar! Even better, as co-writer of 'Picture Of You' he stepped up to receive an Ivor Novello Award, reserved for star songwriters of the Elton John/George Michael variety. Not bad for someone who left school with no GCSEs..!

Ronan also found himself back on stage with fellow pop stars Robbie Williams and All Saints raising a six-figure sum for Irish Childline. But even that was thrown into the shade in March when Ronan Keating turned 21 years of age. That was the excuse for a huge party, a fancy dress bash with *Grease* as its theme. His main present was a Ford Mustang (a sleek American sports car) which he was soon showing off to all and sundry as he and Keith led the St Patrick's Day Parade through Dublin. It was Stephen's birthday, coincidentally – so why wasn't *he* on board? Ill in bed, poor dear!

Happily, young Mr Gately was well enough to accompany Ronan to Japan for a promotional visit late in the month, but someone had got their calendars crossed because the pair both managed to miss group member Shane's wedding to Easther Bennett. On the other hand, maybe it was a hangover from the Vernie situation…

April saw Ronan hopping on stage again – twice! First was with the famous five for another birthday party, Andrew Lloyd Webber's 50th, while Gary Barlow was happy to invite our boy up to duet with him when the ex-Take That man's first solo tour reached Dublin. Even better, 'All That I Need' deposed Run DMC as it crashed in at Number 1 – the third chart-topper of Boyzone's career.

The merry month of May was when 1998 really caught light for Ronan and Boyzone. Inspired by Shane, perhaps, he got married – but this was no whirlwind romance, more like a long drawn-out courtship. The lucky girl was Yvonne Connolly, the shopkeeper's daughter he'd met many years before – and, while he'd gone off to become a pop star, Yvonne had become a top fashion model.

The pair had lost contact for years, and when they met up again they were content to be best friends for a year-and-a-half. But it got much deeper than that, Ronan explained, "to the point where I either had to tell her that I loved her or walk away and never see her again. I chose the first option – because I knew in my heart it was right." And, luckily, the lady felt the same!

Though the wedding took place in exotic climes – on the Caribbean isle of Nevis, where the couple enjoyed an instant honeymoon – Ro had popped the question back home in Dublin. "I really wanted to do the whole thing properly," he explained, "so I got down on one knee for her." Breaking thousands of hearts in the process… Now, he gushed, "I am deliriously happy and this is the greatest moment of my life. We're just *made* for each other."

Home for the happy couple was to be a house outside Dublin which Ronan had moved into the previous Christmas and where he had spent most of the year having garages and gates built and doing all you need to do when you want a mansion fit for the King of Pop and his blushing bride. The pair planned to fill it with "at least 18 kids" – well, that was Ronan's view, anyway – and, while they waited, spent much of their time riding horses, one of the hobbies they shared. With Yvonne modelling and Ronan on tour, the problem was simply going to be finding time!

Boyzone's progress wasn't to be halted by such a small matter as marriage, and a mere week after he'd got himself hitched the globetrotting Mr Keating was to be found across the other side of the world, where he had an engagement to fulfil at the Monte Carlo music awards. Then it was back to launch *Where We Belong*, the Boyz' third album which knocked Simply Red off top spot in the listings. By the end of the year, it had clocked up 30 weeks in the charts and sold a million copies in the UK alone.

As if all that wasn't enough, Shane's kid sisters Keavy and Edele were sitting pretty atop the charts as half of all-singing, all-dancing four-piece B*Witched. Their very first single, 'C'est La Vie', shot into the charts at Number 1 in June with much *Riverdance*-style jigging and an energy that put even the Boyz in the shade!

It hadn't all been smiles, though. The year of 1998, otherwise such a happy 12 months, had brought early heartbreak in February when Ronan's beloved Mam Marie lost a long and painful battle against cancer. At least marrying his childhood friend, three years his senior, had given the youngest Keating the consolation of a soulmate – and when the couple's first child, a son they named Jack, was born on March 15, their joy was unconfined.

"I really wanted to do the whole thing properly, so I got down on one knee for her"

The Boyz enjoyed two more big hits in '98 – 'No Matter What', from the Lloyd Webber musical *Whistle Down The Wind*, gave them their fourth chart-topper in August, while the soulfully-crooned ballad 'I Love The Way You Love Me' ended the year in style with another Number 2 hit. If only Cher had been a dear and moved over!

Amid all this success, Ronan was being tipped as a future solo star by those in the know... even if he consistently took care to deny the rumours! Maybe the critics' habit of putting two and two together and making five had something to do with his two best friends in music outside of Boyzone's ranks. Both ex-Take That star Gary Barlow and one-time Wham! man George Michael had made the transition from teen heart-throbs to adult entertainers... and Ronan, who confessed he was "on the same sort of wavelength, and very much good friends" with Gary, clearly had it in him to do likewise.

Even though he was at pains to stifle those 'split' rumours, it had been clear for some time that Ronan was the best equipped of the five Irishmen for life after Boyzone. He'd flexed his Ivor Novello-winning songwriting talents still further by penning a tune for the Carter Twins, a duo managed by his brother Ciaran, while early 1999 found him putting a toe in business waters himself by becoming co-manager of up-and-coming combo Westside.

"I wanted to give somebody the benefit of my experience," he explained. "I've seen a different side of the business that Westside don't know about yet and hopefully I can teach them things." They could take further lessons from the Boyzone bio-film, due out in April 1999, which was due to tell the story of the world's biggest boy band from Day One.

His career as TV host was coming on apace, too. The BBC offered him the chance to present *Get Your Act Together*, a showcase for promising unsigned artists screened in spring 1999. He gratefully accepted, choosing it in preference to a dating show called *Singled Out* due to its music-based format. The plan was that singers of groups selected by Ro from demo tapes would be teamed with a record producer, stylist and choreographer – then given 48 hours to come up with a potential hit record!

Talking of hits, Boyzone's long-awaited 'Greatest Hits' was due in the summer of 1999, to be followed by a new record and world tour. Ronan had also cut a duet with glam US country star Shania Twain, 'From This Moment', which sounded like a worldwide smash. Its release might just have started more rumours of a solo career. But no, "I'm not quitting" came the cry in late 1998. So no need to fret *just* yet!

It might be too soon to write a fairytale ending to the Ronan Keating story, but the events of early 1999 were enough to a bring a tear to the driest eye. One year earlier, the Irish town of Omagh had found itself making headlines in the most awful way when a bomb blast designed to sabotage the peace process tore the main street apart. This was a place where more than hearts had been broken: many still bore physical and mental scars, while families mourned the loss of loved ones.

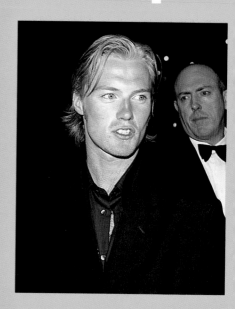

Yet life had to go on for progress to be made, and when it came to staging an event one year afterwards to underline the determination of all peace-loving individuals in the province, there could be only one choice of group – Ireland's finest, Boyzone. Injured and able-bodied alike came to the two shows held in the 1,000-capacity town hall. It was a long time since Ronan and the lads had played anywhere as tiny as this, and they stripped down their show to accommodate the situation, with just backing musicians to accompany them.

But who needed light shows and dancers when Ronan Keating was around, lighting up the stage with his smile? His first words set the scene: "I don't need to go into the reason why we're here… we're here to have a good time, isn't that it?" Ronan had given Omagh permission to enjoy itself for the first time in a year, and the queue of people ushered into his presence after the concert was welcomed equally sincerely. The boy from Boyzone was Ireland's Prince Charming, a man even worldwide acclaim had failed to change. And, after raising £20,000 for the Omagh Fund, his next effort would be the official single for Red Nose Day, a cover of Billy Ocean's 'When The Going Gets Tough, The Tough Get Going'.

Ronan Keating had dared to dream his dream, and now he was living it. "That people will accept me and let me do this is unbelievable, really. This has been a dream of mine since I was a kid and it's actually happened." Here's hoping he – and we – never wake up…

"This has been a dream of mine since I was a kid and it's actually happened"

Full Name	Ronan John Patrick Keating
Date of birth	3 March 1977
Place of birth	Swords, Dublin
Zodiac Sign	Pisces
Eye colour	Blue
Hair colour	Blond
Height	5 feet 7 inches
Lives	Dublin

ronankeating
factfile

Nickname	Tin Tin (at first, because of his haircut), now Ro
Family	Dad Gerry, plus three brothers – Ciaran, Gary and Gerard and one sister, Linda
Qualifications	None: he left school before getting his leaving certificate (Irish GCSE equivalent)
Earliest memory	Falling off a BMX bike he was given as a Christmas present
Favourite school subjects	English (especially drama) and sport
Likes	Designer clothes, cowboy hats and romantic meals
Dislikes	His teeth, rude people, and being away from his family
Favourite drink	Lemsip (for his sore throat)

Big break	Getting into *Boyzone* after three auditions
Career	Joined Boyzone from school. More recently, solo TV commitments have included appearing on *Blankety Blank*, helping co-host the Eurovision Song Contest and hosting the European MTV Awards
Future ambitions	To keep on singing and have his own solo career when the band are no longer around
Hero	Ciaran, his eldest brother

Most embarrassing moment to date	Forgetting one of his dance moves during a big gig in Dublin
Most used word/phrase	"Absolutely!", "God bless ya!"
Favourite place	New York, "Especially Central Park in winter"
Interests	Running, swimming and car racing
First record bought	'Last Christmas' by Wham!
Favourite recent song	'I Believe I Can Fly' by R Kelly
Biggest high in Boyzone	The first Number 1, 'Words'
Dream woman (apart from Yvonne, of course)	Filmstar Michelle Pfeiffer
Favourite TV programme	None – "I prefer to watch movies"
Favourite mode of transport	Harley Davidson motorbike

The fans have put me where I am, so I have to give them as much as I can back. I don't understand people who make a fuss about signing autographs – it's not much to do in return, is it?

I'm scared of losing my voice, particularly on stage. Every singer fears getting nodules on their vocal chords. I don't even want to think about that!

Showbusiness is the best business for me to be in. Everybody has a role in life, and this is what I'm here to do. I love getting up in the morning knowing I'm going to a job I love very much. Not even a job, it's my life.

Sometimes, like when I presented the MTV Awards, I was standing on stage thinking, "Am I really doing this?" But you have to take everything in your stride and not lose your head.

Obviously I was bold, every child is bold, and I did naughty things. I can't say I was a perfect child.

If I'd never joined the band then I would never have found in myself the confidence I feel when I'm on stage and when I meet people now.

I was always the kind of person who liked to take control of a situation, ever since I can remember. I was the leader at school. I never tried to take that role on myself, it was just the way I was seen and the way things worked out.

Music is the language of the world. Everyone understands it, no matter what language you speak.

Until Boyzone I was never very dedicated to anything. I hated school, I was a bit of a wild one. The only thing that ever held my interest was drama. That's why I knew I had to join Boyzone – it was fate calling at my door.

I regret my awful Tin Tin haircut, and ever saying I was a virgin. That's haunted me. But maybe people will forget it now that I'm married!

I look at pictures of myself five years ago and think, "How did I ever wear that?"

I love what I do. I must admit I'm not a fan of photoshoots, though – they're the one thing I don't like, a whole day in front of the camera, It does my head in pulling all those poses, but interviews are fine.

Fame hasn't taught me anything because I don't pay any attention to it, you know? The job has taught me to open my eyes to everything and see what really goes on.

The most famous person I've met is George Michael. I've always admired him, so meeting him was amazing. We speak on the phone sometimes, he's brilliant.

I often talk to God at night and before a concert, and I would love to say I go to Mass every Sunday, but it wouldn't be true – and my mother taught me never to tell a lie.

I am the worst joke teller in the world! I just can't do it! I get them round the wrong way and they don't make sense, but I think they're hilarious. I'll be laughing away but no-one else'll know what I'm going on about!

I spend half my life being embarrassed at what's happening to me. I'm almost permanently shocked by the upfront activities of some of the fans. They'd eat you alive.

I think it's terrible when you see girls sleeping on the streets just to be near us, but you can't tell them to go home, even if it's freezing because then they think you don't want them around. You just have to accept it.

I don't get scared very easily, but occasionally something will send a shiver down my spine, especially if I'm watching a scary movie. That feeling when you sit on the edge of your seat and wait for someone to jump out of the darkness is brilliant.

I don't think I'm good-looking; in fact I think my nose is disgusting!

I like to think of myself as an open person – I think I invite people in.

People have always said that I seem old, even before I was in the band.

I try to do the right thing by people as much as I can. I try never to tell lies, but I'm only human, know what I mean?

I try to remain calm in scary situations. We've had a couple of hairy moments in aeroplanes with emergency landings.

I'm always scared that being in a pop band will turn me into a bighead or give me a bad attitude, because you see so much of it in this business.

I believe in ghosts. Who knows where spirits may end up? I believe because I'd be afraid that if I didn't they'd come and haunt me to prove it!

Love is one of the most wonderful things you can find in the world. There's nothing better. It picks you up when you're down.

Love's when you hear her voice and your legs go weak, or when you see her and your stomach turns upside down. The most wonderful feeling is when you hold someone and know they're going to love you forever.

If you love somebody then anything is possible and because I come from a good Catholic family, I've been raised to respect sex.

I'd never sacrifice my family, not for anything. They are the most important and sacred thing in my life.

Music was my first crush. I was always too interested in sport and music to have a girlfriend.

I love wrapping up in big scarves, coats, gloves and jumpers, and sitting in front of open fires.

Acting would be great, but I don't want to get too sidetracked. I really enjoy presenting, but I don't want to be seen as a presenter. I'm a singer and songwriter, and I want to be taken seriously as that.

I bought a Harley Davidson motorbike and I love it. I wear a helmet and sunglasses and no one know it's me. The mobile phone's in my pocket but if it rings I can't hear it.

I never knock anybody. Everybody tries their best to be something and it's not fair to knock them

You see so many young girls pushing babies around and it's wrong. There's no way they're ready emotionally to deal with something like that when they're still at school.

"What you see is what you get. I'd say I get my honesty from me mam and my soft manner from me dad"

In this industry people tend to forget very easily, and if we disappeared for a while it wouldn't take long to slip from people's minds, especially with all the new bands around.

I was very naïve in the beginning and I had an awful lot to learn, but I kept my ears open, listened to everyone and never said a bad word about anyone. It's a lot different maturing in this business than maturing in college, believe me.

When fans come up to me and say they want to sleep with me, I just laugh and say "Nah, you don't." It's embarrassing.

I don't believe in regrets. I'm a religious person: God has set out a path for me and that is the road I am taking.

If I want something I go for it and I don't stop until I get it! I'm the sort of person who likes to be in control of things – I like to be on top of a situation.

I don't believe in fortune tellers. I believe in God – I'm religious, not superstitious.

I like having power – not over people, but over myself. To know I can take control of a matter gives me a feeling of power. I don't like feeling I'm not in control of myself or my situation.

I don't really ever lose my temper. If I ever feel I'm about to, I take a step back and walk away. It's just very rare that I'll get angry. I don't fight with people or shout at them. I'm pretty straightforward. I tend to say what I have to and then go, "Okay, let's drop it now."

I tend to lock my emotions away and say nothing. I can put on a smiley face if I have a problem. In our business you're better off doing that at times.

At the end of the day, you have to understand that doing interviews is important. It all goes with the job. Some people reckon it's actually therapeutic and I tend to agree – it's quite soothing!

Everybody is made to be the way God intended. I wouldn't want to be anybody else because I'm so lucky.

I have never tried drugs and never will. I watched *Trainspotting* once and that's the closest I've ever come to drugs.

I'd like to think a mate would call me generous, trustworthy and genuine.

I don't see myself as a sex symbol. It's the media who do that, not me! I just get up in the morning and act the way I've always acted. I like to look good – but I don't stand in front of the mirror going "Cor, you're nice!" That's not my thing.

When it comes down to it everyone's human and nobody's perfect. No-one is as squeaky-clean as the media want to make you out to be.

I'm always totally faithful. It's number one on my list. I wouldn't like a girl to do the dirty on me, so I wouldn't do it to her. Honesty and trust is so important – without them a relationship is nothing.

Nobody knew about the wedding, apart from Yvonne and myself. I told my brother Gary as well, and he came to the wedding, but that was it.

Being successful has taught me to respect life, that the simple things in life are often the best – it's true that the best things in life are free.

Everyone knows the pop industry is very fickle. People forget easily. Look at Take That, people have forgotten them already. I can't understand why... they were a great band.

I need to spend a certain amount of time on my own to think things through. People think I'm a bit of a dreamer at times!

I don't think the Millennium will change a thing, although it'll be something for people to talk about for a couple of weeks. It'll be just another year.

My drug is performing. When you stand on stage and look down on all the fans it's such a thrill. It's a real rush and a buzz.

I'm not scared of growing old, at least I try not to think about it. You have to respect age rather than fear it, although the idea of losing my hearing is frightening.

Singles

**Working My Way Back To You/
Father And Son**
Released May 1994 (Ireland only). Highest (Eire) chart position: 2

Love Me For A Reason
Released December 1994. Highest chart position: 2

Key To My Life
Released April 1995. Highest chart position: 3

So Good
Released August 1995. Highest chart position: 3

Albums

Said And Done
Released August 1995. Highest chart position: 1
Tracks:
Together
Coming Home Now
Love Me For A Reason
Oh Carol
When All Is Said And Done
So Good
Can't Stop Me
I'll Be There
Key To My Life
If You Were Mine
Arms Of Mary
Believe In Me
Father And Son

ronankeating
boyzone discography

Father And Son
Released November 1995. Highest chart position: 2

Coming Home Now
Released March 1996. Highest chart position: 4

Words
Released October 1996. Highest chart position: 1

A Different Beat
Released December 1996. Highest chart position: 1

Isn't It A Wonder
Released March 1997. Highest chart position: 2

Picture Of You
Released July 1997. Highest chart position: 2

Baby Can I Hold You/Shooting Star
Released November 1997. Highest chart position: 2

All That I Need
Released April 1998. Highest chart position: 1

No Matter What
Released August 1998. Highest chart position: 1

I Love The Way You Love Me
Released November 1998. Highest chart position: 2

**When The Going Gets Tough,
The Tough Get Going**
Released TBC. Highest chart position: 1

A Different Beat
Released December 1996. Highest chart position: 1
Tracks:
Paradise
A Different Beat
Melting Pot
Ben
Don't Stop Looking For Love
Isn't It A Wonder
Words
It's Time
Games Of Love
Strong Enough
Heaven Knows
Crying In The Night
Give A Little
She Moves Through The Fair

Where We Belong
Released May 1998. Highest chart position: 1
Tracks:
Picture Of You
Baby Can I Hold You
All That I Need
Must Have Been High
And I
That's How Love Goes
Where Did You Go
I'm Learning (Part 1)
One Kiss At A Time
While The World Is Going Crazy
This Is Where I Belong
Will Be Yours
Good Conversation
You Flew Away
I'm Learning (Part 2)

Bonus tracks on reissue:
No Matter What
I Love The Way You Love Me